Whispers Between Silence and Light
Thirty Moments of Love and Self-Discovery

Whispers Between Silence and Light
Thirty Moments of Love and Self-Discovery

Prasanta Behera

BLACK EAGLE BOOKS
Dublin, USA | Bhubaneswar, India

Black Eagle Books
USA address:
7464 Wisdom Lane
Dublin, OH 43016

India address:
E/312, Trident Galaxy, Kalinga Nagar,
Bhubaneswar-751003, Odisha, India

E-mail: info@blackeaglebooks.org
Website: www.blackeaglebooks.org

First International Edition Published by
Black Eagle Books, 2025

WHISPERS BETWEEN SILENCE AND LIGHT
Thirty Moments of Love and Self-Discovery
by **Prasanta Behera**

Copyright © Prasanta Behera

All rights reserved. No part of this publication may be reproduced, stored in a retrieval system, or transmitted, in any form or by any means, electronic, mechanical, photocopying, recording or otherwise without the prior permission of the publisher.

Cover & Interior Design: Ezy's Publication

ISBN- 978-1-64560-756-4 (Paperback)

Printed in the United States of America

*To the voices
and silences
behind the moments —
I am grateful.*

CONTENTS

I. Whispers of Awakening   13
A whisper rises from stillness, a flicker of self, seeking its first breath.

1. A Sacred Sound   15
2. Water's Soul   17
3. The Thread of Gratitude   19
4. The Dust Within Me   21
5. Frost and I: A Winter's Reflection   23

II. Whispers of Dreams and Time   25
Dreams echo through the folds of memory — what was, what is, what lingers between.

1. Dream: Connection   27
2. Dream: Prayer   29
3. Dream: Awakening   31
4. The Dots Now Connect   33
5. Echo of Self   36
6. Space Between Numbers   38
7. Between Heartbeats   41

III. In the Heart's Shadow   43
Love lives in echoes — in glances missed, in laughter held, in silences unnamed.

1. Love   45
2. Conscious Love   46
3. Unfinished Story   49

4.	Life Is Stranger Than Fiction	52
5.	Laguna Nimez	54
6.	Lighthouse	56
7.	Where Whisper Lingers	58
8.	First Yawns, Forever Love	61

IV. The Fading Echo — 63

Memories fade but leave behind their weight — an afterglow of what we carried, and still do.

1.	In the Winter of Life	65
2.	Stumps	67
3.	Hangers	69
4.	Lady Liberty's Silence	71
5.	The Song of Love	73

V. Whispers of the Earth — 75

Mountains, rivers, and wind — they speak in a language older than words.

1.	Wings Over Silence	77
2.	Dusted Trail	78
3.	Patagonia	81

VI. Final Whisper: The Quiet Within — 83

At the edge of thought, there is no self — only awareness watching itself vanish.

1.	The Path Within	85
2.	Echoes of the Mountaintop	86
3.	Nameless Spirit	88
4.	I am the Ocean	90
5.	Whispers Between Silence and Light	92

Preface

Within these pages are moments of reflection—thirty-two poems, each a quiet pause in the flow of life. Three of them, a series on dreams, unfold as a single, continuous journey, carrying you deeper into the spaces between thought and feeling.

May these poems walk beside you in solitude, open windows to the unseen, and remind you gently of the beauty that lingers in each pause

Prasanta
Dec 2025

before the first whisper...

There is a space
between silence and light—
not quite absence,
not yet form—
where breath listens
and the heart speaks without sound.

This book was born in that space.
Not in thunderous moments,
but in soft arrivals:
a glance,
a wave's hush,
a memory that returns in dreams.

The poems within
are not answers,
but traces—
footprints across snow
melting into stillness.

You may find them waiting
in the pause between thoughts,
in the reflection on a train window,
in the murmur of leaves at dusk.

Some will linger like old friends.
Others may vanish
like a bird startled into flight.

But all are offerings—
from one soul to another,
walking together
between silence and light.

April 2025

Section I:
Whispers of Awakening

A whisper rises from stillness, a flicker of self, seeking its first breath.

A Sacred Sound

A winding road ascends to a sacred space,
Where Lord Shiva dwells in timeless grace.
Here, in Srinagar's hallowed air,
Shankaracharya once stood in prayer.

A sanctuary of solace, a tranquil retreat,
Where silence and spirit gently meet.
Hiking up the hill alone,
I found this quote, etched upon a stone:
"Earth has music for those who listen."
Temple bells rang, their echoes wide,
But I sought no chants, nor sacred rite.
I was quietly trying to listen—

The rustling of leaves,
The whispers of wind,
The fluttering of birds,
Songs of Earth, a nature's hymn.

I closed my eyes, and let the quiet descend,
As Earth's symphony began to blend.
Subtle vibrations, in the morning light,
A hush of wonder, a touch of grace.
A moment of oneness, soil and sky,
A whisper of peace as time drifts by.

The Earth's music, both wild and wise,
Plays on the strings where wonder lies.
And in that stillness, I understood the call—
To hush the mind, surrender all.
To listen not just with ear, but soul,
To find the earth's rhythm, in this sacred place.

Feb 2025

Water's Soul

I ponder as I watch—
an artist's vision carved on the New Jersey shore—
a statue, her head of white marble dust,
gazing out toward the Hudson's endless flow.
A finger pressed to her lips,
whispering, *"Silence."*
On the plaque, *"Water's Soul"* etched in stone.
Sunrise sparkles behind Manhattan's towering heights.

Her marble gaze whispers to me,
through waves that ripple not just water,
but the quiet depths of being.
Is she asking for stillness—
to feel the warmth of dawn,
the cool breath of the wind,
the soft pulse of the river's waves?

The sunrise spills gold across the river's skin.
A quiet wind stirs the breath of dawn.
Water murmurs secrets beneath my gaze.

I close my eyes,
let the gates within me swing wide open,
to touch the soul of the water.

*"Listen to the river—it will tell you
what you seek,"*
the boatman once spoke
to Siddhartha, long ago.

I stood,
letting its pulse become my own.
The waters whispered stories long forgotten,
until I, too, began to dissolve.

I close my eyes again,
and float upon the river's song,
dissolving into its depths.

A hush surrounds me.
I feel the water's soul—
silent, eternal, whole.

Only light remains—
no river,
no self.

January 2025
(Inspired by a statue on the River Hudson's waterwalk)

The Thread of Gratitude

Time given,
not time lost—
a fragile thread
in life's great weave—
unraveled,
yet found.

Sometimes days cascade,
and I do not hear—
the steady heartbeat of kindness,
like wind-chimes,
near,
yet unclear.

Anxious thoughts unravel,
whispers raw and wild,
weaving shadows through beauty,
like a lost
and restless child.

Yet gratitude weaves
through each passing hour,
a pattern emerging:
in darkness,
still power.

Each moment shared,
each memory sewn—
a tapestry of longing,
of love we've always known.

Gratitude lingers,
soft as the hush of morning,
tracing light through sorrow
with a tender, golden blush.

I bow to the weaver,
to silence,
to sound—
in gratitude's hush,
the infinite is spun.

Feb 2025

The Dust Within Me

"You are not a drop in the ocean. You are the entire ocean in a drop."
—Rumi

Many poems of Wordsworth, Yeats, and Frost
Reverberate in my head, their meanings embossed.
Yet Meher and Dinkar lie quiet, unheard,
Their echoes silenced—not by choice or word.

Books by Coelho, Frost, Tolstoy rest—
companions whose wisdom pressed.
But Premchand, Mohanty gather dust—
witnesses to a silence I left untouched.

I've studied Washington, Franklin, and Jefferson,
Tracing their struggles, their bold progression.
Yet Nehru and Bose, their passion, their fight,
Linger like whispers just out of sight.

A child of the soil, yet untethered, I roam,
Straying from stories that shaped my home.
The sacrifices of many, the battles they braved,
Echo faintly in the life they saved.
Lately I wrestle with thoughts that confound,
Caught in a maze where my roots feel unbound.

Is this the weight of age, or truth drawing near—
The spirit awakening, breaking through fear?

I seek my roots beneath layers of dust,
Where history sleeps and memories rust.
To feel the earth that carried their pain,
To stand where they stood—in sun and in rain.

Their voices rise from forgotten pages,
From unsung songs and neglected stages.
This battle within is not to divide,
But to reclaim my place with quiet pride.

Let the dust not bury, but teach me to see—
The roots I return to are rising in me.

(*1) Refer to the poetic brilliance of Meher or Dinkar.
(*2) Premchand or Mohanty, custodians of the native narrative.

Frost and I: A Winter's Reflection

"On a snowy winter day —
I have miles to go..."
I could only imagine your words,
As I lived beneath California skies,
Where warmth bathed the earth,
And snow was but a story passing by.

But then, one winter, I found myself
In New England's quiet grasp —
Snow caressing the earth,
Bare trees whispering against the cold,
Train whistle piercing the blizzard's howl.

I have felt your poem before,
Only in the soft echo of my thoughts.
Now, in the comfort of this train,
I feel it in my bones — the chill, the weight,
The road ahead uncertain and long,
While mine is bounded by the tracks,
Confined, yet endless.

I feel the chasm of doubt,
The urge to leave the rails behind,
To walk as you did,
Through the snow-dusted afternoon,

To take the road less traveled,
Though it feels like a reckless dream.
What you wrote—
You chose the path of mystery,
With miles yet to go,
And though I only imagined your journey,
Now, I understand more clearly.

In the quiet of this snowy afternoon,
I read your lines again,
To remind myself of the uncertainty I chase,
But it is in the unknown, the emptiness,
Where I find you,
In every word,
Whispering how to live with the silence,
The empty spaces between steps.

January 2025

Section II:
Whispers of Dreams and Time

Dreams echo through the folds of memory—what was, what is, what lingers between. In this space, time bends, and the self wanders between yesterday and tomorrow

Dream: Connection

I had a dream—most nights, I do.
Some stay with me; some slip away.
Random thoughts scattered
in the shadows of imagination.

Recently, I dreamed
I was dreaming a dream from the past.
I stood in both dreams at once—
like a quantum particle
moving back and forth,
trying to weave the old with the new,
echoing one another.

A strange phenomenon.
A stranger feeling.
I was in both dreams,
at once.

I hovered between them—
the dream of before and the dream of now—
mirrored in a gorge of silence.

I saw myself:
a tear falling in the dream of past,
peace settling in the dream of now.

Vested,
I searched for the thread that bound them.
Two words drifted between the dreams,
superimposed,
like shimmering particles.

I was in both dreams.

Time sculpts time.
Time sculpts dreams.
Time is the thread.
And dreams—
they keep arriving.

I found myself
in the dream of past and the dream of now.
I felt the breath,
and as I woke—
I smiled.

I dreamed a dream
of dreaming itself—
both distant and near,
both then and now.
I woke in wonder,
grateful to be
held
in both.

2024

Dream: Prayer

Walking slowly along the trail,
you paused to watch the twilight—
leaves dancing in the hush of dusk.

You closed your eyes,
breathed deeply,
and in that silence,
you shared:

You'd had a dream—
a dream while I hiked the Himalayas.
Startled, you sat still,
and in that stillness,
a prayer formed—
a quiet rhyme against the wind.

The power of prayer is strange.

Unseen threads
stretched across the sky.
On the same day, in those mountains,
I thought of you.
The glacier's breath,
the hush between peaks—

your name touched the silence
like snow falling on stone.

A dream had connected us.
A thought had reached across miles.
And prayer had kept the journey whole.

Dreams and thoughts—
they move in intertwined epochs.

I hope I'm in your dreams again.
I hope I linger in your prayers.

For even if only for a moment,
you were with me,
and I with you—
until the end.

2024

Dream: Awakening

Dreams arrive—
splintered, piercing
the ravines of darkness.
They lift me for a moment,
then leave me—alone,
within the silence of the dream
where I exist—
alone,
with the dream.

I see a hand, folded
in the mist of sleep—
still, serene,
yet my heart
races toward unseen corners.
Is she telling a story
of forgiveness?
Or offering thanks
for some unseen grace?
Or is it a farewell
slipped beneath the veil of sleep?

A soul half-lit,
half-shadowed—

twilight flickering
within the fold of self.
Flowers fall slowly—
twisting, floating like dew.

Does it matter?
Ashes or petals—
falling
from folded hands
into the sea.

I am in the ravine.
I am in the ocean.
I am the dream.

2024

The Dots Now Connect

In 1986, I saw—
for the first time—
Maradona dribbling,
weaving through defenders,
a blur of brilliance.
It was exhilarating.

A decade later,
I heard *Don't Cry for Me, Argentina*.
Madonna's voice echoed,
but my longing was louder.
The dust of home
had not yet settled.

Two decades later,
I read Neruda's love songs,
searching for myself
in the whispers of yellow & red leaves—
complex, yet deep.
A connection was forming.

Five years later,
Patagonia appeared
on a flickering screen—
Towers of Paine, jagged, poetic.

I yearned to stand beneath them.

Two years later,
Fitz Roy called to me,
like my mother's voice—
gentle, insistent.
No reason—
only the inevitable pull.

One year later,
I made my plans—
to walk alone,
to meet the silence.
Excitement stirred like wind in the valley,
but hesitation followed, too.
Would I still go? Could I?

Six months ago,
A whisper came — a granddaughter on the way.
Joy bloomed, but so did doubt.
Could I still go—
into that unknown,
alone, again?

One month ago,
I held her in my arms,
whispered my question.
She smiled—
small, knowing, infinite.
I understood.

And so, I came.

I found the silence,
the void, the love—
in the mountains of Torres and Fitzroy,
by glacier lagoons,
beneath the southern sky,
through the vast Atacama.

Thank you, Argentina and Chile.
What began fifty years ago—
a dribble, a song, a poem, a longing—
now I see how the dots connect
across this cosmic map.

April 2025
Argentina and Chile

Echo of Self

The ripple reminds me of memory,
its gentle dance across the surface,
a fleeting echo of stillness disturbed.

The wind reminds me of breath,
whispering secrets through the trees,
an echo of breath—unseen, yet deeply felt.

The light reminds me of the sun,
its enduring glow, the rhythm of life,
casting shadows, stitching light,
guiding the day and chasing the night.

Conscious experience—
joy and pain—
echoes of existence,
the pulse that quickens,
the infinite spaces between heartbeats.

They remind me of you:
your presence like gravity,
steady, unyielding,
anchoring my wandering soul.

But as the ripples return to stillness,
and the wind folds into silence,
the truth is reflected:
You are I—
and we are but waves
on the same endless sea.

Jan 2025

Space Between Numbers

I see you lost in thought every day,
head down, in deep meditation.
A quiet rhythm,
putting numbers in Cancan.
You lift a finger: Do not disturb,
when I try to reach you,
met with silence—
a world of numbers where I don't belong.
I wonder...

If I were a number,
would I fit neatly in your box?
Which number should I be
to claim your attention
while you're absorbed in your world of numbers?

One ("1")
I am the one and only for you.
I hope that is true—
A solitary light, steady and bright.

Two ("2")
I exist between two sides,
Like everything in the universe—

The good and the bad,
The joy and the sadness,
Your love and your anger.
Two poles, yet I remain —
between your warmth and your storm

Three ("3")
Three phone calls connected us —
From strangers to friends,
From friends to lovers,
From lovers to a drifting river.

Four ("4")
Bounded by four walls,
A home we built,
With laughter, tears, and quiet nights.

Five ("5")
Five fingers entwined with yours,
Holding on tightly —
A promise unspoken yet known.

Six ("6")
Six times you've steadied me —
when the world tilted,
your hand found mine —
guiding me through the storms.

Seven ("7")
Seven steps we took together,
Sacred vows echoing still.
With every step, I found you again.

Eight ("8")
Eight moments frozen in time,
Echoes of laughter and quiet sighs.
An unending thread that binds us,
Twisting into infinity—our forever.

Nine ("9")
Nine, the circle unbroken,
Where all things converge, then fade—
A dance of beginnings and ends,
I am you,
And you are me.

Zero ("0")
And then, there's zero—
The circle where we begin and end,
In the silent rhythm of love,
Endless, unspoken, whole.

I may not be in your world of numbers,
But I am the silent pulse in your life,
Counting on love,
One or ten,
Zero or infinity.

Jan 2025

Between Heartbeats

My heart murmured, "I am with you,"
but struggled against the tide of emotions.
I feared my silent thoughts
rippling across the emptiness
would disturb the stillness you sought,
or perhaps, I was a forgotten soul,
lost in the shadows of your dreams.

A chasm between thoughts;
spurts of agony, a struggle within.
Yet my heart yearned like a dewdrop—
to share all that I was, from afar,
to let my existence be known.

Yes, I did break your silence—
and maybe I am damned for it.
But I remain oblivious,
for in that moment,
I let the heart speak,
and left the rest to the almighty.
Now, time has softened that ache—
I no longer search for answers
where silence once reigned.
The ripples have faded,

and I've learned to live with the quiet,
and learned—
that even silence
can be heard.

March 2022

Section III:
In the Heart's Shadow

Love lives in echoes—in glances missed, in laughter held, in silences unnamed. Here, each poem is a shadow of tenderness, where presence and absence entwine

Love

Curve of love
Revealed in twilight
Women or Mountain.

Feb 2022

Conscious Love

"Some currents run deeper than sight."

I watched you once—
the way your eyes caught the light,
the rhythm in your walk,
the way silence settled around you.
Then a small breath:

Something stirred in me,
a fascination, perhaps—
the kind that, in youth,
whispers promises it may not keep.

But something deeper moved below,
quiet, unspoken.
A current
not yet named.

Not all rivers seek the sea.
Not all journeys end in union—
Ours meandered.
The current within me faded—
not abruptly,
just slowly,
into sand.

They say the Sarasvati still flows,
beneath the earth,
invisible but not absent.
So too, that feeling—
quietly enduring.

Time passed,
and the earth shifted.
Stillness came.
Then the wind.
Then a whisper of breath:
What the storm revealed
was not ruin,
but roots.
Something had always been there,
waiting to be known.

I walked toward the water's edge,
unfamiliar with my own depths.
There,
something shimmering—
not a form,
but a presence,
a pulse,
a quiet understanding.

Even if the echo was mine alone,
that's alright.
I will wait,
where mountains meet the sky,
in silence,
open to the return of a sound.

I still wonder,
at times—
why certain faces remain
long after footsteps fade.
No answer ever stays long.

But I know this:
Some things begin before we notice.
Some feelings outlive the moment.

And beneath it all,
the current continues—
steady,
unseen,
real.

It was always there,
and remains still—

conscious
love.

May 2024

Unfinished Story

We met again in the meadow,
afternoon sun caressing the mountains.
"Tell me your new stories since last," I ask.
You laugh like birds circling the lake,
echoing across the shimmering waves.

"My stories aren't as exciting as yours;
you tell me—
of your travels,
your hikes among silent hills,
fleeting thoughts in one-minute pictures,
your next book taking root,
scattered lines of an unfinished poem.
You have too many to share," you say,
your smile lingering like the breeze.

Yes, there are stories to tell,
thoughts to share—
but when we meet,
all I want is
your endless conversation,
the quiet reflection of your strength,
how you catch beauty in passing,
feel the pulse of conscious thought,

hold the meditative silence,
the occasional touch,
your faint smile woven between moments,
the unspoken promise to continue;
witnesses,
you and I,
and the wind and the meadow,
keepers of the journey.

"You seek the past," you say,
"while I gather the present."
"And yet," I reply,
"the past lives in the present."
The present has roots we can feel—
like twilight, we meet,
intertwined between past and now,
as souls lost and found,
sharing a single, unfinished story,
one we feel in the hush between words.
The cold breeze stirs—
your breath warms the air.

The stories fold into one another,
woven through the spaces we share,
where time lingers between heartbeats.
The meadow holds us,
the mountains bear silent witness,
as we walk in the shadows of this moment.

You speak of dreams that flutter,
and I of thoughts that wander,
yet in each pause, we find our rhythm—

a dance between heartbeats,
where words fall away like autumn leaves.

There is no need to finish the story.
It lives in the quiet touch,
the glance we exchange,
the comfort of knowing
that the journey—unfinished—
is still ours to walk,
side by side,
always.

May 2023

Life Is Stranger Than Fiction

Beneath the amber sky,
in a park where memories breathe,
you sit beside me—
not mine to hold,
yet still a part of me.

A breeze unsettles the quiet.
You say, almost to yourself,
"Life is stranger than fiction."
I nod—
knowing you are right.

What is life—What is fiction?

In fiction, the story ties itself neatly:
love triumphant,
loss redeemed,
a bow on the end of every chapter.

But in life,
love lingers half-spoken,
threaded in silence,
too fragile to name,
too strong to forget.

We are a chapter unfinished,
a paragraph broken mid-sentence.
Yet perhaps that is the truth—
life is stranger,
and more beautiful,
because it refuses to end
where we expect it to.

So let the story remain unwritten.
Let the fiction wait.
Here, in the quiet between us,
is the only ending we need
unfinished.

And as the sun dips, I silently wish—
"Let the fiction remain unfinished,
for the universe to rewrite."

Jan 2025

Laguna Nimez

I wandered the streets of Santiago,
searching for the winds
of Neruda's love songs—
but they never touched me.

The thought dissolved
like sea mist in the morning.

Days later,

near Laguna Nimez,
where the birds keep their quiet,
I meant to follow the trail
curving around the lagoon—
but I couldn't.

I missed your presence—
your pauses,
your gaze lingering
on the slow-winged flamingo,
on the white petals trembling like breath in the cold.

Without you, the path was hollow.

So I drifted
through the streets of El Calafate,
past windows glowing with golden light,
past voices that meant nothing to me,
trying to fill the space you left behind.

Maybe this is what Neruda meant—
love, not in words,
but in the silence after,
in the weight of an empty hand.

March, 2025
El Calafate, Chile

Lighthouse

Have you forgotten
the whisper of waves,
the hush of boats,
the endless blue waters,
the gold of sunset
brushing your hair like wind?
We watched—
the birds,
the waves,
our footprints dissolving
in time's stalled breath;
yet the scent of those moments lingers.

The mist-cloaked lighthouse,
standing between past and present—
as we once did,
between the winds,
between the tides,
adrift yet bound
by echoes of a journey lost.

You may have forgotten,
but I remain—
like the lighthouse,

its keeper,
tending the light of those memories,
waiting, still, for the echo of your return.

August 2022

Where the Whisper Lingers

Did I say anything
since the last time?
Now, when we meet,
your glances are rarer,
your smile seems faded,
your laugh echoes,
bare.
Is it just my fragmented thought,
or are you seeking silence in your search?

Did I do anything
since the last time?
Now, when we meet
under the tree, near the stream,
surrounded by fallen leaves,
you sit across the bench—
where once,
you sat near.
Is it just imagination,
or have the benches grown longer?

Have I stopped paying attention
since the last time?
Now, when we meet,

the stories have grown shorter,
and time—once infinite—
is interrupted
by alerts.
Sunsets used to linger;
now, clouds brighten behind their cover.
Is it just my perception,
or has the journey taken a turn?

I have searched and searched—
words spoken and unspoken,
deeds done
and undone.
I've scoured the heart,
unearthed the soul,
retraced each path
only to find
no answer.
What did I say?
What did I do,
since the last time we met?
In case you haven't noticed:
the wind is still there,
the birds are still there,
the leaves still flutter,
waves still break on the lake.
The *thin places* remain—
for world and soul to touch
My heart still longs—
for the warmth of your breath,
for laughter from the ravines,
for time to pass

like ducks circling the lake,
memories imprinting
in the shadow of emptiness.
I wait.
I wait—
for your glance.

June 2023

First Yawns, Forever Love

Little fingers, little toes,
A tiny sigh, eyes gently close.
You have arrived on this snowy day,
Angels in a white snow blanket
Welcome you softly.

Bundled up, warm and snug,
A sleepy yawn, a gentle shrug.
What could you dream in this new place,
Just 23 hours in this world so far
Yet I have waited, oh so long,
To hold you close where you belong.

Still wrapped in warmth, safe and tight,
I watch you dream in soft moonlight.
9:34 pm — the clock stands still,
You yawn once more, my heart is filled.
I yawn too, a silent thread,
A bond unspoken, yet wholly said.
Your mother laughs, love all around.

February 9, 2025
Grandfather, Jersey City Hospital

Section IV:
The Fading Echo

Memories fade but leave behind their weight — an afterglow of what we carried, and still do.

In the Winter of Life

In the winter of life, what remains?
Memories—fleeting and frail as snowflakes.
When the rhythm of thought slows,
what lingers?

Letters. Pictures. Fragile tapes.
Threads of moments once lived.
If my house were to blaze,
what would I reach for,
hands trembling, heart unsure?

Old albums. Letters.
Fragments of us—
moments etched in time's amber.

Conscious experiences
captured in shadows and light,
whispers of life lived,
opportunities missed—
memory dividends,
all we carry in life's waning chill.

But now, you ask me—
Destroy them.

The letters,
the pictures,
the tapes.

Erase the echoes of you,
the years we wove together.

How will I remember you
when winter descends upon my mind?
When memory wanes to shadow,
vanishing in winter's breath?
You asked me to delete it all—
to destroy the letters, the pictures, the past.
For freedom, you said—
to unchain yourself from the weight of what we were.

Did you mean for me to forget?
To bury the yesteryears in ash?
Yet you remain—
even in the absence of proof,
even as the fires consume.

In the winter of life,
I will hold the trace of you—
unwritten, unseen.

Memories are gone.
And I am alone.

Jan 2025

Stumps

("In quiet, we become ourselves.")

Once, you stood tall—
a steadfast pillar,
anchoring the pier, unwavering, strong.
Boats sought refuge in your sturdy embrace,
while children's laughter wove joy into your grain.

Now, you are but stumps,
half submerged in the tranquil depths—
a shadow of what was,
a remnant of yesteryears,
unspoken, holding the echoes of time
engraved in silence.

Once, I was like your days of yore:
life surged like waves against my shores,
the rhythm of living drowned my whispers.
But now, retired, the noise has stilled.
The hum of the world softens to a sigh.
The tether of "I"—that ceaseless grip—loosens,
thread by thread, my being unravels,
revealing something deeper, something true.

Rooted in solitude, yet free in stillness,
in this stripped-down state, I find clarity—
a universe unfolding
in vast tenderness.

Above me, skies stretch infinite and blue.
Beneath, the waves murmur what's always true.
The earth beneath my feet hums a melody
for those who dare to pause.

I am not diminished, though I am changed.
I am becoming—reshaped by quietude.
No longer confined by what held me,
but defined by the space I now claim as mine.

My steadfast companion,
we share this truth, this profound revelation:

In stillness, life breathes anew—
a life unshackled, lived on our own terms.
We are on the same shore,
as ships pass by
and we remain—unmoored, yet whole.

Feb 2025

Hangers

Hangers—
simple, plastic hangers,
nothing magical,
until one day,
I counted twenty-four,
unused, clustered together
in the closet,
waiting to be used again.

Should I take some,
use them?
A thought came across—
it means clothes,
which I can get rid of,
will hang a little longer.
I chose not to.
Perhaps it's time
to start my own cluster
of unused hangers.

I glanced again—
as if numbers could change
what time had already taken.
A few more minutes passed,
wondering where they might find new use.

But I decided not to disturb them.
The empty hangers remind me
of someone dear,
who grew up and left,
to chart a course on her own.
The dresses, colorful and bright,
that used to hang,
are gone—
but not the memories,
the stories of yesteryears.

I left the hangers
untouched—
a quiet thank you
for the years,
for love,
for my daughter.

June 2023

Lady Liberty's Silence

Sitting in my daughter's apartment
one early December morning,
along the shores of Jersey City,
I watch through the glass—
a soft veil of snow dusts the winding paths,
boats glide through the mist-laden Hudson,
and Lady Liberty rises, bathed in dawn's first light,
facing southeast, as she always has—
a sentinel of welcome,
a promise to those who crossed the sea.

I ask her,
How do you feel?
Do the same winds still whisper in your ear?
Does the sun still warm your face?
What do the waves murmur at your feet?

Silence.
A breath held between the waves.

Do my footsteps still echo on your shore?

Silence lingers.

Two months later, from the same window,
the snow is gone.
The world has shifted—
another headline, another burden.
I sip bitter coffee,
watch as the light bends differently.
Lady Liberty rises once more,
but shadows cling to her shoulders.
The dawn does not reach her face.
Her torch—once steady—
now flickers, uncertain.
Her outstretched arms
no longer seem to welcome the weary.

I ask again,
Are the winds the same?
Do you still feel the sun's warmth?
What do the waves whisper to you now?

For a long moment—nothing.

Then, a voice soft as breaking waves replies:
"I am time's prisoner once more—
why must I stand on this lonely shore?"

Feb 2025
The political winds for immigrants changed on January 10,
2025.

Songs of Love

The Song of Love on FM 98.1,
a tender hum, like a lover's sigh—
faint, yet filling the quiet ride.

A turn of the dial—
songs of God by Pandit Jasraj,
sacred melodies weaving through the air.

Two songs for the soul—
One earthly, one divine,
No difference.

Jan 2020

Section V: Whispers of the Earth

Mountains, rivers, and wind—they speak in a language older than words. Listen closely, and you may hear the earth whisper its truths back to you.

Section V
Whispers of the Dark

Wings Over Silence

Clouds spread beneath me,
Orange light fills the skyline—
Wings shifting shadows.

Nov 2019 (In an Airplane)

Dusted Trail

"Footsteps fade. The path remains within."

Part I – Why
Why for do I walk
on these dusted trails of the Camino?
neither religious
nor heir to a Christian heritage.
What for do I walk
this ancient pilgrim path,
I wonder.

Was it a random thought,
after reading Coelho,
or seeing the story of a father
completing a son's journey?
Or perhaps it is my own—
completing a circle
begun years ago.

It is all of these,
and perhaps more.

Part II – Reflection
I walk alone—
but you are with me,

woven into my dusted backpack,
your prayer strings hanging
beside my quiet thoughts.

I am not walking alone.

Each stone tells a story,
most unknown.
Now and then, a rock,
a tree, a lake, a single flower
comes into view—
and reminds me
of the journey taken
through the dusted years.

I walk alone,
yet never alone,
upon these dusted trails.

Part III – Complete

Facing the sun,
near Santiago de Compostela,
I offer my prayer—
not for miracles,
nor for forgiveness,
but for the simple grace
of having walked this far
of making this pilgrimage.

I bow to the dust, the stones, the sky,
to the silent companions

who walked with me unseen.
I thank the universe—
for the long road,
for the silent lessons,
for the circles closing
and opening again.

I have arrived,
not at a destination,
but at myself.

Sept 2025
Camino Frances, Spain

Patagonia

The sky
The mountains, the glaciers, the lagoons
The Steppes
The wind, the rain, the snow
The sun
The Torres

Laid me bare
to a single thought—

an indescribable thought.

Conscious love.

The dry whisper of steppes
Ice cracking off the glacier
A gust of wind lifts my tent
Rain kisses my cheeks like needles
The weight of soaked shoes
The slow dance of fog—

There was only one thought—
no thought at all.

Where do I belong?
Between the void and love,
I stand.

Silence persists.

March 2025

Section VI:
Final Whisper: The Quiet Within

At the edge of thought, there is no self—only awareness watching itself vanish.

The Path Within

A few Steps...
From uncertainty to beauty;
A few words...
From fogged soul to bliss.

Jan 2022

Echoes of the Mountaintop

Part I
I will keep the fire
burning for you,
from the mountaintop,
I believed you'd need.
and I waited…

Part II
I came down from the mountain
to remind you—
there is a light for you
on the mountaintop,
a light of friendship.
But you had forgotten:
the fire,
the mountaintop,
the light,
the promise—
the promise.
Forgotten.
You had moved on.
And I was left alone,
after all these long years.

An eerie silence followed,
echoing through the hollow grounds
of memory,
where it all began.

Part III
I returned to the mountaintop,
to sit in stillness —
to listen to the wind,
to hear the mountain,
to heed the voice within.
They spoke in unison:

The fire was for me.
The mountain — mine.
The journey — mine.

It was always "I"
on the mountain
and below.

I understood.

I let the fire keep burning.
I let the light shine on.
And I moved forward —
finally at peace.

Jan 2025

Nameless Spirit

I read a line in an email:
"I am vegetarian; I do not drink; I am spiritual."
I paused—
Am I spiritual?

Is it going to a temple,
reciting lines from sacred texts,
offering verses to the silence,
or simply choosing how to live?

Is it one, a few, all—or none?
Is "spiritual" a spark to be declared,
or a flame that burns quietly within?

Does a river name itself
before joining the sea?
Does the wind ask its purpose
before whispering through the trees?

Spirituality—
the nameless flame,
the silent echo inside,
heard only when we truly listen.

We are all spiritual.
We walk our own paths.
No need to declare—
let others see, or not.
It does not matter.

If the universe breathes through me,
must I name the air I inhale?
In stillness, I arrive—
a speck of dust, part of the stars,
a silence that belongs to all,
a flame that does not need a name.

Jan 2025

I am the Ocean

I sit.
Thoughts flicker—
comets slipping across a silent sky.
I reach for one—gone.
Another—vanished
before I can touch it.
Stillness evades me.

"Focus on something,"
 a friend once said.
 So I do.

I imagine the park—
the one where the path curves by the lake.
I'm on the old bench,
water catching the last light of day.
Ripples breathe over grass.
Flowers lean into wind.
Ducks carve quiet spirals in the hush.

I watch.
I listen.
And then—
a warmth beside me.
Not a figure, but presence—
as if the moment itself is sitting here.

My chest opens.
I feel joy.

Then the voice:
Let it go.
This beauty too is a ripple.

So I do.
I release the flowers,
the ducks,
the fading sun,
the bench,
the lake.

When nothing remains—
I become the wave.
No.
Not the wave.
The water.
The depth.
The stillness beneath movement.

Who thought I was a wave?
Perhaps the one still sitting on the bench,
waiting for meditation to end.

But I am not waiting.
I am not one.

I am the wave.
I am the watcher.
I am the ocean.

Watching itself disappear.

Final Poem

Whispers Between Silence and Light

Between the hush of what is gone
and the glow of what remains,
a whisper lingers—
not of answers,
but of presence.

It is not the word,
but the pause before it.
Not the sun,
but the warmth it leaves behind.

Somewhere in that space—
not quite night,
not yet dawn—
you waited.
And I listened.

A breath held,
a glance unspoken,
the brush of wind
through pages not yet turned—
each moment
a thread in the silence.

Love was not loud.
It arrived gently—
riverlight on trembling reeds,
dust remembering
where it once belonged.

I walked this path,
not to arrive,
but to dissolve—
into echoes,
into light,
into the stillness
that cradles everything.

And if you find yourself
standing there too—
between the silence
and the light—
you will hear it:

the voice of the soul,
soft and steady,
whispering—
you were never alone.

--- END ---

Prasanta Behera lives in the Bay Area, California. After more than three decades in the technology world, he has turned his attention to the quieter pursuits of reflection and creativity. An avid hiker and cyclist, he draws inspiration from nature and the rhythm of everyday life. When not on the trail or behind the pen, he enjoys creating children's books that celebrate wonder and imagination. This is his third poetry collection.

Books Published by Black Eagle Books

Children's Books

Poetry Books

Translated Books

Black Eagle Books

www.blackeaglebooks.org
info@blackeaglebooks.org

Black Eagle Books, an independent publisher, was founded as a nonprofit organization in April, 2019. It is our mission to connect and engage the Indian diaspora and the world at large with the best of works of world literature published on a collaborative platform, with special emphasis on foregrounding Contemporary Classics and New Writing.

www.ingramcontent.com/pod-product-compliance
Lightning Source LLC
Chambersburg PA
CBHW060620080526
44585CB00013B/909